The Mean Dream Wonder Machine

Margaret McAllister

Illustrated by Tim Archbold

OXFORD
UNIVERSITY PRESS

For my godson Martin and his brothers,
Aidan, Euan and Joseph.

1

Grotty Monday

Of course I made mistakes. All inventors
make mistakes. Even Professor Scriffle does,
but he doesn't shout about it. My inventions
had a few teething troubles. But they
happened in the wrong place, at the wrong
time.

I don't need to tell you what happened on

..day, do I? It wasn't my fault.

Grotty Monday started my mum
..ghting with the washing machine, and
the washing machine was winning. It usually
did. You never knew if it would start, flood,
creak, dance all over the kitchen or go into
self-destruct and blow itself to atoms.

I'm pretty good with machines. I was
always repairing it but it wouldn't go on
forever, and we really needed it. There are
four of us – Mum, me, (I'm Patrick), my sister
Laura, and little Hannah. She's only three.
My dad went off with somebody else when
Hannah was a baby, and money's been tight
ever since.

So, on Grotty Monday, the old washing
machine wouldn't start. Mum kicked it, and
it rumbled and stopped again. She thumped
it, and the door fell off. I finished my
breakfast and went to fetch my screwdrivers.
Finding the loose connection was easy, but I
had to get most of the insides outside to

tighten it up. Laura was already going out to school.

'If I'm late, tell Mrs Cramp I'm doing the washing machine,' I yelled after her. I finished as fast as I could, and that's pretty fast, but I knew I'd be late for school. I ran full pelt all the way and I was gasping for breath when I got there. I could see everyone having a giggle behind their hands. I went and stood at Mrs Cramp's desk.

She pushed her chair back as if she was afraid of catching something. She had this way of looking at you as if you'd just crawled out from under the sink. 'Your sister tells me you've been mending a washing machine,' she said, very slowly. I heard them all spluttering and making rude noises, trying not-to laugh out loud. I nodded.

'Well, I'm very pleased to hear that you're making yourself useful, Patrick,' she said. 'But I'd rather you did domestic repairs in your own time, not school time.'

I wanted to say that I couldn't mend the thing until it broke down, but I knew better than to chance it.

'Sorry, Miss,' I said. The giggling was getting infectious. I didn't dare look at anyone.

'Go to your seat and borrow someone else's book to catch up,' she said.

I did, but I'd soon finished and I got out my rough book and started brushing up designs for a robot. I like designing things, so I . . . 'PATRICK!'

I wish she wouldn't do that! Mrs Cramp's got a shout like a starting pistol. One leathery hand slapped down on my book. She was prepared to overlook my being late, she said, but not wasting time drawing cartoons. I was in big trouble. Detention at break time. She'd find me a job to do. I supposed it must be cleaning out the cupboard again. It usually is.

When it was nearly break time, I saw her look in the cupboard and pull a face. It was already as neat as an empty box in there. 'There's always the art things,' she said, and stood tapping her teeth with her pen. 'Come here, Patrick.'

There were piles of art paper, some rough, thick sugar paper and some very thin stuff. She complains about it, whatever it is. It's always the wrong size, the wrong colour, and it tears easily. The brushes are too hard, the paint's too thick, the glue's too sticky. She muttered something about making posters and went on tapping her teeth with her pen.

I thought she was trying to play the National Anthem, but then she said, 'Set out the painting things during break, Patrick. At least we can use up that useless paper and that awful paint.'

She was right about the paint and paper. It was rubbish. The paper tore as soon as you picked it up, and the paint was so thin, you could have watered the garden with it. It needed something to make the paint stronger. And the paper, too.

I like solving problems.

Glue might help. There was some wallpaper paste in there, a bit old and lumpy, but I thought I'd try it. I tipped a bit into each pot of paint and stirred it in, then I spread some paper on the floor and gave it a very thin layer of glue. I wanted to see if it would soak in and stiffen the paper as it dried out. But while I was doing that, something happened to the paint in the pots.

It had gone a bit – um – soupy. Lumpy in

places and watery in others, and it was
getting lumpier
even while I
watched it. The
yellow was
starting to harden
round the edges and
bubble up in the
middle – have you
ever seen custard boil
over in the microwave?

I grabbed the brushes and started stirring
like mad, but as I was stirring one pot, the
next one was going lumpy. I needed to stir
them all at once. I was looking in all
directions at once for anything I could use,
and still stirring with a brush in each hand.

I tried tying five paint brushes
together, but they weren't long

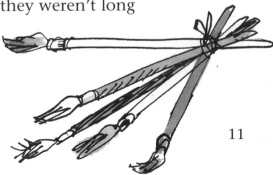

enough, so I got another five and tied them
to those to make five double-length brushes. I
taped them together at the top, so I had a
five-pronged, extra-long paint brush. It
worked, but it was so long I had to climb on
the desk to use it. I had to keep changing
hands, because it hurt my arms. And while I
did that, I kept an eye on the paper.

No way would it dry in time for the next
lesson. I needed to hurry it up. There was an
electric fan in the cupboard so I fixed that
up, just on the lowest setting, to blow air

over the paper without wafting it away. It was working, too, and I was standing on the desk stirring and trying to work out how I could rig up a motor for the paint brushes, when I heard the door open.

'PATRICK!'

Mrs Cramp. And the whole class.

'Patrick Penn! What do you think you're doing?' snarled Mrs Cramp, and marched in. She should train Rottweilers.

'I'm stirring paint,' I said. 'Try not to walk on the paper, it's –'

'This paper's covered in glue!' she screamed.

'It's covered in glue,' I said. 'I tried to tell you, Miss.'

She got off it pretty sharply, and stepped out of her shoes so as not to spread it around. All the rest of the class were in by then. Our Laura was coming in with some books for Mrs Cramp, so she stopped to watch.

'And what's this fan doing here?' she

demanded, and bent down to switch it off. She pressed the wrong switch. The fan shot into full power and let out a draught like a force eight gale.

The whole sheet of sticky paper rose up from the floor and wrapped itself around Mrs Cramp, Emily Cook, and all of Tom Binney's reading group. I jumped down to unwrap them, but the rest of the class got there before me. Laura had the sense to turn the fan off, but by then there were bits of sticky paper all over the floor, and kids slipping in it, and sticking to each other, and Tom Binney might

have had a really bad fall if he hadn't landed
against the fire extinguisher, and it was a
foam one, and by the time it had finished
spraying you couldn't see Mrs Cramp,
and . . .

. . . and then the
headteacher came in to
see what the noise was
about.

2

Scriffle

Our headmaster is called Mr Robinson. He's about the size of a large wardrobe, and he looks even bigger when you're standing in front of the desk in his office, and he's towering behind it. The Chairman of the Governors was beside him – they'd sent for him specially. He'd had to leave his game of golf and he wasn't pleased. Mrs Cramp was sipping hot sweet tea.

I liked Mr Robinson. He looks like a roaring giant, but he's kind and he's fair. He knows everybody's name, and he really cares about everyone, and about your work and whether you're happy at school. I didn't want him to think badly of me.

'School budgets are very tight,' said the Chairman. 'You, Patrick, have just ruined five large tins of paint, ten brushes, and a great quantity of paper. Several children are in a seriously wet and sticky condition, Mrs Cramp is in shock, and the caretaker is still cleaning up the foam. Have you anything to say?'

It wasn't easy but I tried to explain that I was trying to help, not just mucking about and being stupid. Mrs Cramp and the

Chairman looked bored, as if they'd heard it all before.

'I think this is a clear case for suspension,' said the Chairman. 'Shall I telephone Mrs Penn, or will you, Mr Robinson?' My face

burned scarlet, and I looked at the floor to try and hide it.

'I think we should all calm down,' said Mr Robinson. 'Sit down, Patrick.' He opened a cardboard file on his desk, glanced at it, folded his hands and spoke to me. He took no notice at all of Mrs Cramp and the Chairman. 'Patrick, you've done some very good work in this school, haven't you? Especially in science. That's your favourite subject, isn't it?'

I nodded. I knew Mrs Cramp was ready with an earful of stories about how I'd spilt iron filings on the floor and broken the handle of the desk pencil sharpener, trying out my experiments.

'I think you have great ability, Patrick,' he said, 'but it needs to be trained and organized. Have you heard of Professor Scriffle?'

My head jerked up. Professor Scriffle! I said yes, I'd heard of him. He works at the university in town, but he's famous all over the country.

He invented the Ultra-Vid machine, that plays videos and serves up drinks and ice creams half-way through. And the Scary Hairy Dryer that dries your hair, perms it, and changes its colour at the same time. He's done really important work for hospitals, too, designing equipment for laser surgery. He's the best.

'Professor Scriffle,' he said, 'is running a summer school for three weeks during the holiday. It's for young people who show talent in science, engineering and maths, the people who might be the inventors and engineers of the future. There are a few free places available, I believe. Are you taking this in, Patrick?'

'Yes, sir,' I said, and I wondered what he was really saying. I didn't dare to hope, but I couldn't help it either.

'I think it could be just the thing for you, Patrick,' he said.

The Chairman sort of growled, and Mrs Cramp spluttered into her tea and sprayed it all over the carpet, but Mr Robinson held up his hand.

'If Patrick is determined to invent things, he may as well learn to do it safely,' he said,

'and he has talent. We must make the most of it. Professor Scriffle wrote to me to ask if I have any pupils I want to recommend for the summer school, and I thought of Patrick and Laura Penn. Patrick, I am prepared to ask Professor Scriffle to give you a place on the summer school, but there's another side to this. You behave yourself for the rest of the term. No more turning up late, no more scrawling diagrams in your rough book, and certainly no wrecked classrooms. Somebody could have been seriously injured.'

'Yes, sir. Sorry, sir. Thank you, sir.' My face was trying to smile, but I didn't dare let it. Mrs Cramp was cross enough already.

'Good. Now, apologize to Mrs Cramp for all the trouble you've caused, then scarper.'

'Sorry, Mrs Cramp,' I said. I left the room very meekly. As soon as I was out of the door I jumped up, punched the air, hit the ceiling. I couldn't wait to get home and tell Mum – and, yes, I did want to tell her everything, including what happened at break. I didn't want Laura getting in with her version first.

I ran all the way home. There was Mum, wringing out the washing by hand.

'That machine's finally had it,' she said wearily. 'It did a final spin and exploded. Take care how you go into the kitchen, the floor's still a bit wet.'

A bit wet! Hannah was in her bare feet, paddling. There was a pink sock draped over the kettle and a pair of knickers hanging from a saucepan, and the cat had got tangled up in purple pyjamas as it raced for the cat flap. Laura arrived, and we rescued the cat, dried the floor and picked up the bits of washing machine. We found the door in the vegetable rack. The drum was still in one piece, but it wasn't round any more. It was sort of triangular. Hannah put it on her head and said it was a helmet. All the other bits went in the bin.

It was a good thing the window was shut when it happened. There'd be bits of twisted metal and a Winnie-the-Pooh nightie orbiting Jupiter forever. Mum came in with a brave smile, and said she'd work all the extra hours she could until we could afford a new machine. In the meantime, we'd have to do the washing in the bath.

After that, it seemed a bit of an anti-climax when I told Mum about the summer school. But when she heard, she closed her eyes, smiled broadly and said, 'Patrick, that's the best thing that's happened to us for months.'

That made me even more determined to stay out of trouble. Laura had the same idea. She never left me alone with a pot of glue, a battery or a screwdriver. She hung around when I was doing my homework to make sure it was done properly. At the same time, she seemed to work incredibly hard herself.

At the end of term, Mr Robinson stood up in assembly and said that two pupils with 'outstanding ability' were going to the Scriffle Summer School. 'Patrick and Laura Penn,' he said.

The idea that Laura was going too made me angry at first, but I was pleased, at the same time. The summer school was my thing, my bit of triumph, and she'd pushed in on it. But at least there'd be one familiar face there. If we got lost, we could get lost together. It helped.

But we didn't get lost. We turned up together on the first day of the summer school.

3

Mean Dream Washing Machine

We took the bus to town, then walked to the university. We had to find the Research and Development Unit, which was a lot of shoebox-shaped buildings at the back. The other kids all seemed to know each other. They were chatting about all the other courses they'd been on. Laura and I played

Hangman on the back of my exercise book until Professor Scriffle walked in, and everything went quiet. He looked as if he'd got dressed with his eyes shut. He was tall and thin, with short grey hair and a beard. His jacket was buttoned up wrong, his trousers didn't match it, and he was wearing odd socks. He looked at you over his glasses as if his eyes were X-rays and he could see right through you, but they were kind eyes. Sometimes he got his words mixed up, like the time when he said we needed to 'explode' (he meant experiment). It was as if he was so enthusiastic, he just grabbed whatever word was nearest. I think he did the same thing with his clothes when he got dressed in the mornings. He told us about what we'd be doing, then he took us on a tour of the workshops.

I could tell you about all the things in those workshops, but you wouldn't understand how I felt, walking from one miracle to another. We started off looking at little things, like the Thermal Chip Trip. It's a bag to put your chips in, and however long it takes you to get home and eat them, they're still hot and crisp and taste as good as they did when they were first dished up.

There were binoculars that could see round corners, so bird watchers can see the spuggies when they hide behind a bush. Then there were sound and colour machines that play music and project moving pictures on to your walls, and a party machine that fits into the ceiling and sprays bubbles and confetti. There were useful things, too, heart monitors and security systems.

In the last room we went to, there were the household machines. I was ready to be bored, like you are when you have to go with your mum to buy a vacuum cleaner. All the washing machines were being used, but they all ran very quietly.

There was one large, gleaming white washing machine standing alone on a platform. Above it was a chart with Professor Scriffle's name on it, and dates of when tests had been carried out. The professor went up to it, looked it up and down with something like love, and ran his hand along the top as if he were stroking a pet.

'This,' he said, 'is the Mean Dream Washing Machine.' He stroked it again. 'It is my . . . what could you call it . . . ? My . . .'

'Cat?' I suggested, but nobody

heard me and Laura stamped on my foot.

'My baby. My dream. My great work.' He gave a great big smile, and held out his hands as if he expected the washing machine to jump through a hoop. 'Do you see, at the

 front it has a video screen! Nobody likes reading instruction books, so this one has an

instruction video!' He put a tape in the slot and his face popped up on the screen, telling himself how to work it. It was brilliant, it was all computerized, with a coffee machine thing on the top.

'It will wash anything,' he said happily. 'It fluffs up cuddly toys, it brightens colours, it leaves your clothes dried, aired, folded and ready to wear. And we test all machines very thoroughly, so we know that they can take rough treatment. This machine is doing the laundry for a whole troop of Boy Scouts after a week's camping in Yorkshire. As you watch, it is handling three pairs of trainers, twenty-one highly dangerous socks, and a sleeping bag.'

He took one more look at it as if it was his best ever birthday present, then he said, 'To work! To work! Today, we start with the basics. Over the next three weeks we will work our way sideways, diagonally, and up.'

In the mornings at the summer school we had classes, and in the afternoons we'd work on our own designs. I was in the lab that led to the washing machines room. In the evening, of course, Laura and I went home and helped with the washing. On wet days, there was half-dry washing everywhere, draped over Hannah's Play House and Mum's exercise bike.

Everybody at the summer school had to choose a project of their own. We had to think of an invention, design it, build models of little bits of it, see what went wrong. Some people did games machines, some did motorized

skateboards or intruder alarms that trapped burglars in a net. Laura was doing a robotic rocking horse.

I had a stunning idea. A hovercraft for going to the beach. It would skim down to the shore and over the sand, and you could take it on land and water, and all without getting sand in your packed lunch. I loved it. I called it the Sea Storm Flyer.

There were always staff around to help us, but Professor Scriffle himself checked everyone's designs. It was Friday by the time he saw mine, and when he called me into his office I thought I was in trouble. I usually am.

I sat down. Something barked, and I jumped up again.

'Don't worry, that's just an alarm system I'm working on,' he said. 'Sit down, Patrick.'

My designs lay on his desk. My Sea Storm Flyer! I desperately wanted him to like it. There was a report, too, in Mr Robinson's handwriting, and I was trying to read it upside down when Professor Scriffle said,

'This is a very interesting report from your headmaster. And your designs for the Sea Storm Flapper – sorry, Flyer – yes. Yes.' He looked at me over the top of his glasses.

'I think, Patrick, you could be a remarkable inventor. You are full of bright ideas, but you have to learn to take one step at a time. If you cover paper with glue and put a fan

beside it, it's going to flap and stick, isn't it? And if you pour glue into paint, isn't it best to try it one pot at a time, to see what happens? Take one thing at a time, Patrick, and always think things through.

'I had to make sixty-eight different adjustments to the Mean Dream Washing Machine before it was exactly right. But I do like your idea very much. Start with a small, battery-operated model. If you like, you can come in here on Saturdays and do a bit of extra work.'

'Oh – wow – oh – I mean – um – thank you, thank you very much, sir!' I babbled. Free use of the labs. Wow!

All the way home I felt I was in the Sea Storm Flyer, racing along the sands. Professor Scriffle was pleased, he liked my designs, he was letting me go in on Saturdays!

I found Mum up to her knees in washing.

'Hannah's been painting,' she said. 'She got it everywhere. Chair covers, curtains, everywhere.' It was the first time I'd ever seen Mum look defeated. Everything was going so right for me, and so wrong for her.

'No problem, Mum,' I said. 'Leave it to me.'

4

The joozy

'Are you sure this is all right?' said Mum, as I went out in the morning with a holdall full of washing.

'Fine,' I said, trying to sound certain. 'There are loads of washing machines at the labs. That's what they're for. Washing.'

I didn't tell her that the washing machines were Professor Scriffle's newest prototypes. She didn't need to know that. And he wanted the Mean Dream Washing Machine thoroughly tested, didn't he?

At the lab, I put the instruction video into the Mean Dream Washing Machine, and I watched it really carefully. This was Professor Scriffle's favourite machine. I didn't want to do it any harm. Think things through, one step at a time, that's what he said.

The technology in that machine was so advanced, it was way ahead of its time. I loaded up the washing, switched it on, and went into the lab next door to work on my model. One of the lab assistants looked in, but he just said, 'Are they still testing those machines?' I nodded, and went on working.

Mum was delighted when she saw the clean washing. She was like the mothers on those washing powder adverts, when they hold out the rugby kit and it's so gleaming white you need sunglasses. It made such a difference, not having damp washing everywhere.

'Any time, Mum,' I said.

Laura gave me a bit of a look. When Mum wasn't there, she said, 'Have you cleared this with Professor Scriffle?'

'Professor Scriffle's cool,' I said, and changed the subject. How could I do anything else? Mum was so happy. And what if I'd asked Professor Scriffle, and he'd been angry with me for even asking? I didn't want him to stop being pleased with me.

I had a good day at the lab on Monday, and came home to find Mum talking on the phone to someone. She put it down and crossed a name off a list.

'I can't find a baby-sitter,' she said. 'The boss wants me to work afternoons all this week. We need the money, but there's nobody to take Hannah.'

I didn't think. I just said it.

'She can come with us.'

'Of course she can't!' said Mum.

'Patrick!' said Laura.

'Yes, please, very much,' said Hannah.

'Don't be ridiculous,' said Mum. 'Professor Scriffle wouldn't allow it.'

'I'll sort it out with him,' I said, as if he

and I were best mates. 'Bring her to the gate at half past twelve.' Laura tried to interrupt, but I ignored her. 'Just for tomorrow, then you'll find a babysitter for the rest of the week.'

I really, truly meant to ask Professor Scriffle if it would be all right. But when I went in that morning, I heard him on the telephone giving an ear-bending to somebody who had sent him a faulty part for a machine. He was livid. It didn't seem like a good time to ask a favour. So I didn't say anything about Hannah. She could play quietly in the room with the washing machines. Nobody ever went in there in the afternoons.

When Mum and Hannah arrived they'd just been to the library. She'd got out the video of *The Lion King*, and had it tucked under her arm.

'Great,' I said. If the Mean Dream Washing Machine could show an instruction video, it could show any video.

It was a doddle of an afternoon. When Mum was stuck again on Wednesday, I said I'd take Hannah again.

Hannah was red-eyed and sniffing on the Wednesday. She thought she was going to the swimming pool – she usually does on Wednesdays. She even had her little cossie with her, and a drink for afterwards. She sat watching Professor Scriffle's video, and rubbing her hand across her eyes.

'I wanted swimming,' she sniffed. 'I was going in the joozy.'

'The what?' I said. I was trying to concentrate on the Sea Storm Flyer.

'The joozy,' she said. 'The wibbly tickly bath thing.'

'The jacuzzi!' I said. My model was coming on beautifully. I was trying to remember everything Professor Scriffle had told me, but it was difficult with Hannah sniffing next door in the washing machine room.

'Let's have a look, then,' I said. I lifted the lid of the Mean Dream Washing Machine – it opened from the top – and checked out where the hoses were. The drying cycle was supposed to blow hot air into the machine. If I could teach it to do that when the machine was full, but not running . . .

You couldn't do it with an ordinary washing machine, but this one had safety devices so the motor wouldn't run if you even put your hand in it, let alone a small child. I made quite sure she wouldn't get hurt.

I'd already worked out how to get into the computer's memory. I told it how to turn itself into a jacuzzi, and it believed me. I tested it, then told Hannah to put her cossie on.

'Here's your jacuzzi,' I said, lifting her up. 'Don't touch any buttons and don't shut the lid.'

Then the door opened, and I nearly dropped her.

'PATRICK! What do you think you're doing?'

5

One step at a time

'Laura! You scared the daylights out of me!'

'What do you think you're doing?' She was staring as if I'd just invented Frankenstein. It was a silly question. She could see perfectly well what I was doing.

'Professor Scriffle will murder you!' she said. 'If he finds out . . .'

'He's not going to find out,' I said, and lowered Hannah into her jacuzzi. 'At least, I'm not going to tell him.'

'I hope she's safe in there,' said Laura.

'Of course she's safe,' I said. 'And so am I, if nobody tells Professor Scriffle. I'll leave it the way it was.'

Laura looked grim, but she was thinking about it. 'I won't tell Professor Scriffle anything,' she said at last, 'but I'm telling you, Patrick. Get that machine back to normal, sharpish. And if he does find out, don't expect me to help you. It's nothing to do with me. You needn't think I'll stand by you, because I won't.'

She stalked off with her nose in the air, but Hannah didn't even notice. She was enjoying her jacuzzi.

I invented something else that day. You know the Mean Dream Washing Machine had its own coffee maker? Hannah doesn't drink coffee, but she had one of those banana milk shake things with her. She wanted it after she got out and dried off. I put it in the place where the coffee machine went, turned up the spin speed and loosened a screw so the vibration would froth it up.

I was learning to think one step ahead, so I'd poured the banana milk shake into the coffee pot, to give plenty of room for the

bubbles. It was just as well I did. It gurgled and flooped and shook, and by the time I took it out it was more shake than milk. Hannah could hardly see over the top of it.

What a machine! Washer, video, jacuzzi, and maker of the best milk shakes in town! I put it right before we went home.

On the bus, Laura wouldn't speak to me. I didn't care. I was thinking about that machine. I lay awake that night because of it.

We didn't have a computer, but I'd bought a couple of games at a school sale, in case I ever got the chance to play them. The Mean Dream Washing Machine's computer was very advanced, but very simple, too, once you understood it.

Computers do what you tell them. The trick is knowing how to tell them, and I'd already sorted that one.

I wasn't really going to play computer games on it, of course. I just wanted to see if it would work.

I took some more washing in with me the next day, but I had to hide it in a cupboard, because Professor Scriffle started his afternoon rounds with me. He'd just been furious because somebody had sent him the wrong order for batteries, but he was really nice to me. He was as keen on my project as I was! He pointed out a few improvements I could make, but he was pleased with it so far.

I felt guilty about sneaking our washing into his machine. But he wanted it tested, didn't he?

When he'd gone I put the washing in and loaded up a computer game, a football one, to see if it would work. It came up on the screen first time, no problems! I thought I'd better try it, to see if it ran smoothly.

They're really good, these footie games. I had a couple of shots at goal in the first five minutes, but I didn't quite get it in the net, and the second one was just unlucky. It hit the post. That wasn't really fair, so I gave

myself a few minutes more, to have a
reasonable chance of scoring . . . and I did,
and then the other team did, so . . . In no
time, I was on Level Three. I couldn't believe
it when my watch bleeped! It couldn't be
that time! I'd only played a bit of footie. I
hadn't even started correcting the mistakes
on the Sea Storm Flyer! Still, I could work
extra hard the next day, and come in on
Saturday, too.

*   *   *

On Friday morning at breakfast time, Hannah
wanted to come to the lab. We said no and
she sulked a bit, but then a toy in a
polythene packet fell out of the cornflakes
box and she pounced on it. It was only a
cross-eyed plastic penguin, but she thought it
was great. She started chattering on about
toys, and the more she talked, the more I
thought about inventions. Toys and

inventions. I had an idea.

When I was little, I had an electric train set. It wasn't one of those massive ones that take over your bedroom – I wish! It was a small 'figure of eight' track with two engines and a bridge, but when I was a kid I loved it more than anything. I played with it every spare moment I had. When I got older I didn't bother with it so much, because there's a limit to what you can do with a train set when you don't have much track. But I'd kept it, and now, I had an idea.

I'd need to take the train to the lab. I also needed a timer. I'd bought an old cuckoo clock at a jumble sale because I thought it might be useful one day. And I stopped to buy sweets on the way to the lab – little ones, dolly mixtures, choc drops. That kind of thing.

I did most of the work during lunchtime, when I was pretty sure nobody would come in to see the Mean Dream Washing Machine.

I opened all the inlets for soap and fabric conditioner and stuff, and the filter where all the yucky fluffy bits end up, and fitted track into them. I convinced the computer that it was meant to be that way. I fitted the cuckoo clock to the machine's timer, and then . . .

And then it was time to get back to work, in case Professor Scriffle came to see my model. It was looking cool, that model. I'd connected it to a battery, and adjusted it until everything was as smooth as a fish in water. I was enjoying it. After all, that's the sort of thing I'd come to the summer school to do. I never meant to do anything with the Mean Dream Washing Machine.

The door opened, and in walked Professor Scriffle.

'Patrick!' he said. 'This beautiful design. I see you're making a mess, I mean, making amendments to it.' (He was grabbing the nearest word again.) 'Let's have a look.'

Professor Scriffle spent the rest of the afternoon with me, just me, and my Sea Storm Flyer. He didn't try to take over – he just asked the right questions, so I could work out for myself what needed doing. I wanted the Sea Storm Flyer to be really class. I wanted to do well, for Professor Scriffle's sake. And if he knew what I'd done to the Mean Dream Washing Machine . . .

'This still needs a bit of work,' he was saying.

'I'll be in tomorrow morning,' I said, and he was pleased. He didn't know why I was coming in on Saturday. He mustn't know.

After he'd gone, I wondered how I'd got into this. I'd only meant to do Mum's washing. Then videos, then games . . .

I knew I should have gone straight in and taken out everything I'd done to that machine. But I'd come too far for that. I just had to be there on Saturday morning, to see if it worked. When I'd done that, I'd leave the Mean Dream Washing Machine exactly as I found it. I promised myself that, as I went home.

6

Mean Dream disaster

'If I work this weekend,' said Mum that night, 'we'll have enough for a good second-hand washing machine. I saw one for sale on the noticeboard at the supermarket, and I want to get it before anybody else does. I don't like to ask you, but . . .'

'No problem,' I said, 'I'll take Hannah. I was going to, anyway.'

That was part of the fun of adapting the machine. I'd been imagining Hannah's face when she saw it. I had a treat planned for her. She came bouncing onto the bus with Laura and me. We were off to work like the seven dwarfs, but there were only three of us – Grumpy, Jumpy and Guilty. Hannah had a few things in a bag, including her favourite cuddly toy. It's a yellow duck. I can remember when it was new and fluffy, but it had turned a bit grubby and its fur had gone all thick and tufty, the way they do. It's got big goggly eyes, so it always looks shocked. She had that daft plastic penguin with her, too. She danced into the lab and asked about the joozy. Laura was still glaring with a face like a firework, but I thought – so what? I'll just run this machine for Hannah, then I'll put it back the way it was. By Monday morning, I'll be the perfect summer school pupil again. 'Are you ready, Hannah? Look at this.'

'What on earth have you . . . ?' began Laura.

'If you don't want to see it, go,' I said, but she hovered in the doorway. I switched on.

I pressed the button marked 'express', and turned the timer. There was a buzz and a ping, and a door popped open to show the cuckoo clock as it cuckoo-ed six times. (It had lost its cuckoo, but it made the right noise.) Other doors opened, and the railway track rose out from them, unfolded and laid itself round the top of the machine and down the sides. There was a bit of clicking, and then – you know the way you feel when you've given someone a really brilliant present, and you watch them unwrap it? That's how I felt when I saw Hannah's face as she watched what happened next. The engine whirred out of the washing

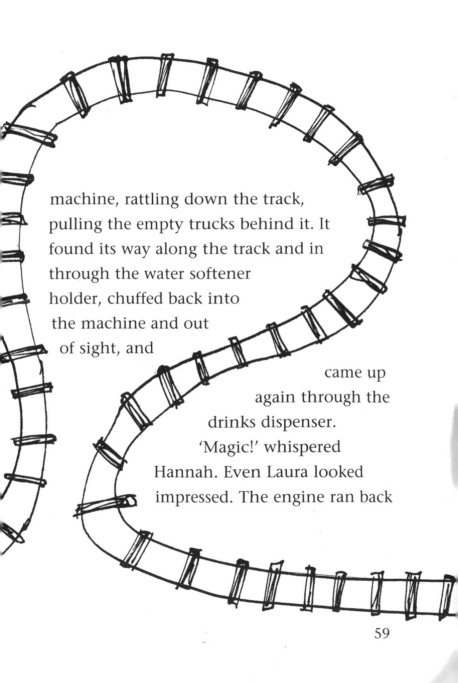

machine, rattling down the track,
pulling the empty trucks behind it. It
found its way along the track and in
through the water softener
holder, chuffed back into
the machine and out
of sight, and

came up
again through the
drinks dispenser.
'Magic!' whispered
Hannah. Even Laura looked
impressed. The engine ran back

into the machine again, and clicked to a halt.

'It's stuck!' said Hannah.

'Watch,' I said.

For a minute, nothing happened. I was wondering whether it needed a thump when I heard a dispenser click open, unload, and shut again. Then the engine purred, the door opened, and out came the express train, with every truck carrying a bright little mound of sweets – dolly mixtures, jelly shapes, chocolate.

'Ooh, ooh, ooh!' gasped Hannah. I didn't know if she was delighted, or doing the sound effects. When she found her voice she said the cuckoo clock needed a cuckoo, and gave me the cross-eyed penguin. It didn't seem to bother her that penguins aren't supposed to say 'cuckoo', so I fastened it to the spring and set the timer. The machine went buzz-ping-cuckoo, the penguin shot out, and Laura and I were holding each other up laughing when we heard footsteps outside.

We stopped laughing as if we'd been switched off.

We dashed into the lab next door and tried to look busy. One of the lab assistants looked in.

'Oh, I didn't think anyone was in today. Professor Scriffle's bringing a visitor round, but they won't bother you. They're just going to look at the Mean Dream Washing Machine.'

'Oh?' I said, and my voice came out squeaky.

'Yes, he's going to demonstrate it to a man called Dr Silver. He's from a big electronics firm. If he likes the design, his company will pay mega-money for the rights to build and sell the machines. Keep your fingers crossed!'

I was doing that already. I stood stone still until she'd gone away, then Laura snapped, 'Idiot!' and I jumped.

Re-programme the computer, that was my first thought. I ran to the machine and tapped and clicked desperately, trying to erase everything I'd done, but panic made me clumsy and my fingers got tied in knots. I took off any track that was showing and tried to disconnect the penguin cuckoo clock, but I'd made it too tight and the screwdriver kept slipping. Laura was re-programming Hannah.

'You've never had a jacuzzi in the washing machine, do you understand, Hannah? If anyone asks you, you've never had a jacuzzi in the washing machine.'

'Never had a joozy in the washing machine.'

'Good girl. Again, Hannah.'

'Never had a joozy in the washing machine.'

I gave up the fight with the penguin

cuckoo clock. There was no way I could get it out, and the train was still inside, too. I jammed the penguin's door so that, if it did go off while the professor was there, it couldn't jump out. There might be a faint 'cuck-whack' as it hit the door, but if everybody kept talking loudly it might not be noticed.

'He's coming,' whispered Laura. I shut all
the doors on the machine, rubbed my hands
dry on my jeans, and hid the screwdriver in
my back pocket, which wasn't a good idea.
We made sure we were in the lab, not in the
washing machine room, when the professor
and Dr Silver came in.

Dr Silver had curly black hair, very neat,
like a poodle that's just been clipped. He
wore a sharp grey suit and he looked like a
bored kid being dragged round the shops by
his mum. The professor had tried to smarten
himself up, but his jacket was crumpled and
he was carrying a bin bag full of washing. He
stopped when he saw Hannah.

'This is our little sister,' said Laura. 'I came
in to see how Patrick was doing, but I wasn't
stopping, because I have to look after
Hannah today, and I can't bring her in here,
can I, except I have, but only for a minute,
and we're just going . . .' she paused for
breath. 'Come on, Hannah.'

Professor Scriffle looked down at Hannah as if she shouldn't really be there, but he couldn't manage to be cross about it.

'That's all right,' he said. 'She won't be any trouble. Now, Dr Silver, in here,' and he opened the door, 'is the Mean Dream Washing Machine. Let me just load up the instructions. It's all on video.'

The right video was in the slot. So far, so good.

'It's not as good as *The Lion King*,' piped up Hannah.

'Shut up, Hannah,' whispered Laura, and slipped her a sweet.

The video ran, and the professor set the coffee machine going. It was a good thing I'd given the coffee pot a good wash.

'Banana milk shake, please,' said Hannah. Professor Scriffle and Dr Silver laughed.

'No, dear,' said Professor Scriffle. 'This machine only does coffee.'

'It does . . .' began Hannah, and then she

said 'glomma glomma ilk shay,' as Laura stuck a huge great toffee in her mouth. The coffee pot gurgled away, and the professor pushed washing and powder into the machine.

'Funny,' he said, 'there's a pink sock in here. I wonder where that came from?'

'I thought you'd been washing for Boy Scouts?' yawned Dr Silver.

'I have,' said the professor. 'They must have changed the uniform since my day. Now, the machine will work out how much washing it has to do, calculate water, time, spin speed and fluffiness, and do the rest. It's fast, and very quiet.'

The machine was quiet, but the coffee pot

wasn't. I'd meant to do another milk shake for Hannah, so I'd loosened the screw. The coffee machine made floopy noises like somebody blowing bubbles through a straw. Professor Scriffle lifted the lid of the coffee pot.

You know the froth you get when you shake up a bottle of Coke? There was loads more than that.

'Cappuccino!' said Dr Silver. 'Cool!'

The professor frowned, and sniffed at it.

'Cappuccino with a hint of banana,' he said. 'I don't understand that.'

Neither did I. I'd washed it. For the first time, Professor Scriffle glanced at me, and looked suspicious. I tried to look innocent.

They both drank the coffee, though, and Dr Silver had a second cup, but he still looked bored. When the washing was finished, the professor called me in to help unload the machine.

'Patrick is one of my star pupils,' he said to

Dr Silver. 'Now, before we open the machine, Dr Silver, you'll see the computer screen flash up the message, "YOUR LAUNDRY IS READY FOR COLLECTION."'

It didn't. It flashed up 'PENN THE STRIKER SCORES AGAIN!!!'

The professor looked down at me. He'd stopped smiling.

'I hope nobody has touched this machine,' he said quietly. 'Especially, I hope nobody has been using it to play games.'

'Can it play games?' asked Dr Silver eagerly. But I think the professor was trying to cover up what had happened. We unloaded the washing, and Dr Silver inspected it and said how dry and soft it was. He was impressed. I hoped he'd seen enough, and they'd go away. My mouth was dry, my legs were shaky, I was losing my nerve. I sat down, and got up again quickly. I'd forgotten the screwdriver.

'You must see the air-fluff setting,' said

Professor Scriffle. 'You'll like this.'

You won't, I thought. You really won't. Please go. Please disappear, or let me disappear, or let the fire alarm go off, or let me wake up from a nightmare.

'I've brought some soft toys,' said the professor.

'Me too.' Hannah trotted up to him with the yellow duck and some teddies and things.

The professor smiled at her, so it seemed Hannah was safe, even if I wasn't. She helped him put them in the machine.

'This machine makes old cuddly toys soft, fluffy, and as good as new,' announced Professor Scriffle. 'That's what the air-fluff setting is for. And it is a great time saver. To speed the process, we simply adjust the timer.'

The timer. The cuckoo clock. Sooner or later, they'd make contact.

'I think we'd better go,' I said, and rubbed sweaty hands on my jeans. 'Hannah, say goodbye to Professor Scriffle.'

But Hannah had practised her line. She wasn't going to leave without saying it.

'Never had a joozy in the washing machine,' she said loudly.

'I beg your pardon?' asked the professor, with a puzzled little frown.

'I never had a joozy in the washing machine,' she repeated, very clearly, to make sure he got it. Professor Scriffle turned the puzzled frown towards me.

'What does she mean?' he asked.

'I've no idea. If we don't go now, we'll miss our bus, won't we, Laura?'

'Duck's in there,' complained Hannah, 'and so is . . .'

'The soap powder!' I said loudly, so the professor wouldn't hear her say 'penguin'.

'In the . . .' She made a great effort, like a acrobat running up for a somersault. 'The JACUZZI!' she said, and she enjoyed it so much, she said it again. 'JACUZZI!'

'She doesn't know what that means,' said Laura hastily.

'I do!' insisted Hannah, pointing. 'That's a ja . . . oops.' She put her hand on her mouth.

The professor turned very pale. Scary pale. He trembled a little, and his eyes were fierce. This was dangerous.

'I hope,' he said, slowly, 'that she does not mean what I think she means.'

'A jacuzzi?' said Dr Silver with interest.

'No,' said Hannah. 'Never had a joozy . . .'

'Be quiet, Hannah, please,' sighed Laura.

She was. In the quiet, we all heard something.

'What was that?' asked the professor sharply.

'IT'S REALLY GOOD, THIS MACHINE!' I shouted, to try and hide the noise.

Inside the machine, the penguin cuckoo hit the door. *Cuck-whack.*

'Is there a bird trapped in there?' asked Dr Silver.

Cuck-whack. Cuck-whack. I started singing

loudly, but the only thing I could think of
was a Christmas carol. Laura joined in.

'Oh, the rising of the sun,' we bellowed.

The professor fell to his knees and
wrenched open the jammed door. He toppled
backwards as the cross-eyed penguin shot out
and hung quivering on its spring. There was
a scream of horror from Professor Scriffle.

'Cuckoo!' said the penguin.

'Cool!' said Dr Silver.

'Help,' whispered Laura.

Clickety-clunk, clickety-clunk, came the sound of the train. I heard it hit the door it should come out of, but I'd jammed it. Not even I knew what would happen next.

7

Suspended!

The professor was on the floor where he'd fallen, shaking with rage. Dr Silver was watching like a kid at a magic show.

Everything went quiet. Perhaps the train had run out of track and stopped. Then it started up again, whirring and clacking. It

grew louder and faster, and from the
penguin's door out rattled the chocolate
express, clattering over the cuckoo clock, over
the penguin, until, at last, it rocked to a
perfect stop at Dr Silver's feet.

'Amazing!' he exclaimed.

'I am so sorry about this, Dr Silver,'
muttered Professor Scriffle. He scrambled to
his feet. 'This is nothing to do with me.'

But the Mean Dream Washing Machine hadn't finished.

It whizzed into the air-fluff setting, and Hannah jumped with excitement. The motor stopped. The lid flipped open and out shot a teddy bear, fluffed up to three times its normal size. Then all the cuddlies catapulted out, whizzing up in all directions like fireworks, rabbits in frocks, a panda and a three-legged sheep, hurtling all over the lab. The sheep flew out of the window, but we caught the rest.

'Where duck?' demanded Hannah. And that duck rocketed into the air, fluffed up like a great yellow pom-pom with a surprised look on its face. It dropped into Hannah's arms and looked indignant.

'Thank you!' she said. She hugged the duck, and then hugged the professor round the knees. He bent down and stroked her hair, but his eyes were on me, burning holes in me, and I couldn't look at him.

'Dr Silver,' he said, 'I am so sorry, but could you wait in my office? Hannah, one of the

lab assistants will look after you. Patrick,
Laura, in the lab. Now.'

*   *   *

I think it would have been easier if he'd
shouted. But he was quiet, like a time bomb
when it stops ticking. 'Have you anything to
say?' he asked. It was like a very soft growl. I
tried to explain, but my voice wobbled.

'I'm sorry. Really sorry. I wish I hadn't
done it . . . I didn't mean to . . . not at first.'

He raised his eyebrows. I knew what he
was thinking. You can't build a train set into
a washing machine and not mean to do it.

'It was just the washing at first,' I said, and
I explained about not having a machine at
home, and having to baby-sit Laura.

'So you put in videos and computer games.
And converted it to a jacuzzi. And a train set.'

'I wanted to see if it would work.'

'You could have wrecked thousands of

pounds of technology and destroyed two years of work. If it had been medical equipment that you fooled about with you could have killed someone. You know, Patrick, that you were nearly suspended from school for your disastrous experiments with glue?'

'Yes, sir.'

'Mr Robinson saw you had potential, and asked me to take you on. I did, because I saw you had the ability to become a great inventor and engineer. But until you learn,' and here he raised his voice, 'until you learn, Patrick, to keep your fingers away from other people's work, you are no use in a lab. You are a danger zone!'

My face was burning. He turned to Laura.

'Well, Laura?'

'It was nothing to do with Laura,' I said.

'I WAS SPEAKING TO YOUR SISTER!' For the first time, he shouted, and banged the table. 'WHEN WILL YOU LEARN TO MIND

YOUR OWN BUSINESS!'

'I knew about it, sir,' she said.

'Please, sir,' I said, cautiously, 'she tried to stop me, but I wouldn't listen.'

He sighed deeply. 'You didn't tell me, Laura.'

'No.'

'She didn't know about it all, sir,' I said. 'Not until the last minute.'

'Patrick,' he said, 'you may clear up your materials. You will not be coming back for the rest of the summer school. I'm sorry about that. Your work was outstanding, and I liked working with you. But this is unacceptable.'

'Yes, sir.' It was all I could say.

'Laura, I think you played less part in this than your brother. You may continue at summer school, but you are under a final warning.'

'No, sir,' she said. 'If Patrick goes, I go.'

'Don't be stupid, Laura,' I muttered.

'This means more to Patrick than it does to me,' she said. 'I can't stay if he can't. It would be cruel.'

Professor Scriffle took off his glasses, rubbed his eyes as if they itched, and put on his glasses again.

'Well, Laura, it's your decision. But I'm sorry to hear it.'

We trudged out miserably, and nearly fell

over Hannah. She was waiting outside, and her duck was so fluffy she could hardly see past it. She rushed to reach up and put her arms round the professor.

'Duck's lovely,' she said. 'Thank you. And you're lovely.'

Professor Scriffle went down on his knees. He gave her a great big bear hug.

'For a lonely old bachelor like myself,' he

said, 'that is very important, Hannah.' Then I think he said something . . . no, it couldn't have been. I think he said something about us being very lucky. I didn't feel lucky. I dismantled the train, and packed up my things. Laura and Hannah were waiting for me.

'I thought you said you wouldn't stand by me,' I said.

She gave me a sweet. 'Shut up and eat that,' she said.

I didn't want to tell Mum, but Laura said we had to. First she went ballistic, then she marched into her bedroom and banged the door, and I think she cried, but we didn't dare go in. Later, she said we had to write a proper apology immediately, and she wrote one, too, and we had to take them straight to the post box.

I tried to write what I meant, but how could I? He'd been so kind, and he was just so brilliant. He wasn't like anyone I'd ever

met. Now I'd disappointed him, messed up his invention, and shut myself out of his world. Sorry wasn't enough.

You might want to know if I cried. I don't have to tell you that.

8

But . . .

The phone rang on Monday morning when we were hanging around and wondering what to do, now we weren't at summer school. Mum answered it.

'Professor Scriffle wants to see you both,' she said. 'And me, too. We'll have to take Hannah.'

'Do you think he might let us go back?' I whispered to Laura.

'In your dreams,' she said. We were sent straight to Professor Scriffle's office. When any of the assistants saw us they pointed and whispered. Professor Scriffle was at his desk with a file open in front of him, and I could see it was about the Mean Dream Washing Machine. He introduced himself to Mum, and showed her to the only armchair. His face was still stern. I'd seen him being kind and patient and I'd seen him in a rage. Now, I just couldn't tell what was coming.

'Thank you for your letters,' he said. 'I don't wish to go over all the events of Saturday again, but, Patrick, there is something I need to know.'

'Yes, sir?'

'Why didn't you ask me if you could use the machine for your family's washing?'

'Because . . .' Oops, I thought.

'Because you thought I would say no?'

'Yes, sir.'

He sighed. 'So you knew that what you were doing would not be approved of, but you did it anyway. If you had asked me, Patrick, I would have said yes.'

Oh, fiddle, I thought. It was a bit late now.

'I still mean everything I said on Saturday. But . . .'

He seemed to change into someone else. He leaned across the desk with excitement shining in his eyes.

'Dr Silver phoned on Saturday night. He loves the machine! He wants to buy the rights! He thinks it's wonderful! But he means the machine as he saw it, Patrick. Train, games, the lot. He's called it the Mean Dream WONDER Machine. I've taken it apart and put it together again, and I can't figure it out.' He seemed to have forgotten all about Saturday, as a smile of delight spread across his face. 'It's amazing! How on earth did you do it?'

So I showed him, and he was fascinated. He pointed out a few mistakes, too. I'd loosened screws so that the machine vibrated too much, and the drinks machine could have overheated and been dangerous. He was

right, I did have a lot to learn. At last, he said, 'You are expelled from summer school, as you know. But you can get yourself along here every evening and help me with this machine!'

'Yes, sir!' I said.

'Laura!' he said. 'Get to your class.'

'But sir, I'm expelled.'

'Get to your class! When will you two learn to do as you are told?' Then he peered into the machine, and I couldn't see if he was smiling.

When it was time for us to go, he shook Mum's hand and said we were a remarkable family. Then he turned to me and said, 'You'll hear soon about the contract.'

'Contract?' I said.

Apparently, Dr Silver's company was going to pay him tons of money for the Mean Dream Wonder Machine. And half the work was mine, so half the money would be paid to me.

'Oh, and . . .' he waved at one of the lab assistants, 'sort out one of the prototypes of the Mean Dream Washing Machine and have it delivered to Mrs Penn's address. An early version will do, so long as it has the cuddly toys programme.'

'Thank you very much, Professor Scriffle!' said Mum. 'And, Patrick . . .'

'Don't worry,' I said. 'I won't touch it.'

*   *   *

We still see Professor Scriffle a lot. He calls so much, I think he fancies Mum, and that's all right with me. We work together on lots of projects, but he insists that I learn the basics, step by step.

Now and again, though, we do some work on my own project. We've nearly built a prototype. Then we'll have to test it, alter it, improve it, test it again – it'll take a long time, but one day, at last, it'll be launched. It'll be real. My dream. My own Wonder Machine. My Sea Storm Flyer.

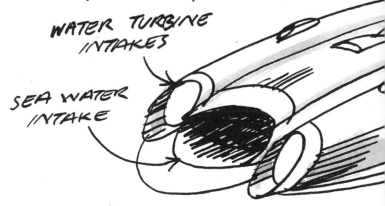

WATER TURBINE INTAKES

SEA WATER INTAKE

SEA STORM FLYER

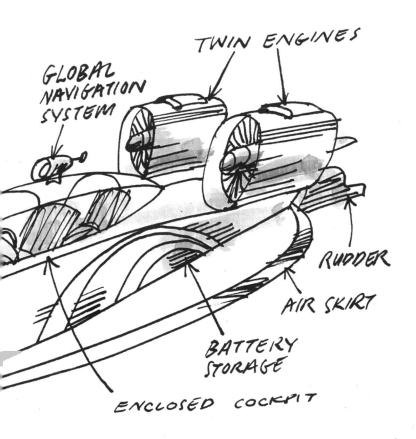

TWIN ENGINES

GLOBAL NAVIGATION SYSTEM

RUDDER

AIR SKIRT

BATTERY STORAGE

ENCLOSED COCKPIT

About the author

Last year, we moved house. That meant a week of unpacking battered old tea chests and wondering which one I'd put the teapot in, and at the same time there was all the usual work to do, like washing. I wished I had a machine that could do all the washing, dry it, fold it, iron it and put it away . . . and perhaps it could make the coffee as well . . . and show videos . . . and play games . . .